Low-Fat Cooking in Clay

Full Flavor the Subtle Way

Contents

Fundamentals

Recipes

Appendix

Low-Fat, Light, and Wonderfully Flavorful

You've seen them before but tell the truth, when was the last time you cooked in a clay pot? This is just about the most nutritious low-fat cooking method available, and ideal for today's health and figure-conscious cooks. Clay pot cooking is always flavorful and nutritious because cooking in it requires hardly any fat at all. Whether you prepare vegetable, meat, poultry, or fish dishes, everything cooks in its own juices and retains the delicious, natural flavor intended. It's the best tasting way to lose your fat!

3

The Benefits of Cooking in Clay

Simplicity

For most recipes, you can prepare and load all the ingredients in the clay pot at once. For some dishes, you'll need to brown, blanch, or precook ingredients beforehand. After a few basic steps though, you'll simply set the cover on top and stick the whole thing in the oven.

Free time while cooking

There's no need to keep checking and testing food once it is in the clay pot; the food is enveloped in heat and cooked with the steam that forms once the clay pot is sealed. There is also no burning or sticking. Until the timer rings, your time is your own.

Low-fat and vitamin-rich

You can eliminate most or all of the fat. Usually you need no more than a little butter, olive oil, cream, or cheese to finish the flavors and maximize the health benefits of fat-soluble vitamins. Although the oven is heated to 400°F, the evaporating moisture in the clay pot regulates the temperature at about 210°F. This causes the ingredients to cook slowly, which means they retain their vitamins and minerals. And since none of the aroma can escape, the flavor of the food becomes concentrated which allows you to use salt sparingly.

Nothing but the best taste

➤ Vegetable dishes

All vegetables can be cooked in their own juices. You don't throw away any water when you're done, therefore you don't lose any vitamins, minerals, or flavor. For $1\frac{3}{4}$ lbs vegetables, add about 2 cups liquid (either water or stock).

➤ Soups, stews, and casseroles

When braised in a clay pot, the flavors of ingredients are blended in a natural way. You can finish a soup by puréeing it with a hand blender right in the pot. If you want your casserole to have a nice crust, simply remove the cover toward the end.

➤ Meat, poultry, and game

You can cook a whole roast, pieces of meat, or poultry medallions slowly with a little liquid (wine or stock) and onions or vegetables. Everything becomes tender and juicy because the moisture is locked in—a few extra minutes won't make any difference as the food does not dry out.

➤ Fish and seafood

Fish also cooks in its own juices and stays beautifully tender. A clay pot made especially for fish also lets you cook larger fillets or whole fish. If you want a whole fish to form a crust, remove the cover during the last quarter of the cooking time.

➤ Bread

Bread turns out particularly well in a clay pot. You can bake loaves in a standard clay pot or in a special bread baker without a cover. When baking without a cover, place a small container of water in the bottom of the oven to increase the humidity and form a nice crust on your bread.

The Clay Pot Family

Clay pots are made of porous clay. The bottom and top are the same size. The bottom is coated with a special glaze and is easy to clean, while the top is unglazed. Both pieces have wide edges that fit together. A small gap between the top and bottom sections helps regulate the pressure inside the clay pot and allows excess steam to escape. The ridges on the bottom of the clay pot's interior prevent direct contact between the liquid and food during cooking so that all sides can brown evenly—provided it isn't surrounded by vegetables or other ingredients in your recipe.

Standard clay pot

Available in four sizes: 2–4 servings; 4–6 servings, which is the most popular size; a large clay pot for roasting a turkey or goose; the maxi-clay pot for roasts of up to 18 pounds.

Clay pot fish baker

This shallow clay pot designed for fish is an easy, natural way to cook any variety of whole fish or fillet. If you prepare fish often, this is the one to use because the pores in the clay absorb the fishy taste.

Bread baker

It's best to have a separate clay pot for desserts or bread because the unglazed top gradually absorbs odors, which will add to the flavor of your breads or sweet pastries over time.

Variations

You can purchase a designer clay pot from any number of kitchen and home stores. If you love skewers, there's also a clay pot with a spit so you can cook vegetables and skewers at the same time.

Cooking in Clay

Soak the pot

Soak the top and bottom in cold water for 10 minutes before using them—longer for extended cooking times.

Cook with the cover

Normally the cover remains on during cooking to keep the ingredients from drying out. But you can make roasts, casseroles, and breads that have a crust if you briefly remove the cover toward the end of cooking.

Place in a cold oven

Always place a clay pot on a rack in a cold oven, as close to the center as possible. Then turn on the heat. If you have

> **1** **Soak the clay pot**
> The pores in the clay fill up with water and then release the moisture during cooking.

a gas oven, start at the lowest temperature and gradually raise it.

Cooking times

The times stated in this book are approximations. Temperatures and heating-up times can vary greatly from oven to oven so the first time you use a clay pot, check whether the dish is really done at the specified time. It won't hurt the food if you leave it in the oven a little longer.

Hot or cold— no, thank you!

Clay pots are sensitive to temperature changes and can crack or break. So remember:
➤ Place the hot pot on a cake rack or trivet to cool.
➤ Never set the pot on a hot burner.
➤ Never pour cold liquid into a hot pot.

Cleaning the pot

Wash the top and bottom like any other pot, rinse in clear water, and soak if

> **2** **Capacity**
> Never fill a clay pot all the way to the top to keep it from overflow during cooking.

necessary. Clean the clay pot well before using it for the first time to make sure the pores are open. Remove any residue as described under Troubleshooting. After cleaning, let the top and bottom air dry thoroughly.

Storing your clay pot

Reverse the cover and place it in the clay pot. Store in a well ventilated place.

Troubleshooting

Too much or too little cooking liquid

➤ If too much liquid formed while the dish was cooking, you can pour a little out and use it for another sauce or soup.

If there isn't enough liquid, bring a little stock to a boil in a separate pot and pour the hot stock over the food or stir it into the ingredients.

Cooking times are too short

➤ Sometimes a roast or turkey isn't as done as you'd like it to be due, perhaps, to temperature fluctuations or the quality of the meat. In this case, put the top back on and cook it in the oven for another 20–30 minutes.

And if the vegetables are still too firm, just keep cooking. If part of your meal appears to be cooked but your meat does not, pull out the cooked vegetables, keep covered in a bowl or pot, and add back to the clay pot for the last five minutes of cooking.

The sauce is too fatty

➤ This mainly happens with poultry when the fat under the skin escapes during roasting. There are several methods for reducing fat in a sauce:

Pour sauce into a fat separator (a pot with the spout attached at the bottom). The fat rises to the top and you can pour out the low-fat part of the sauce through the spout.

Remove fat from the sauce with paper towels or a ladle.

Let sauce cool and remove cold fat.

Cooked-on food

➤ Just soak the clay pot a little longer and then you'll be able to remove it easily with water and a dish brush.

Fish odor

➤ Does your clay pot smell like the fish you last made in it? Put a little vinegar in the dishwater and this will take care of it.

The clay pot wasn't clean to begin with

➤ If the clay pot starts to smell musty or even molds after sitting for a while, fill it with vinegar water and heat it in the oven at 400°F for 1 hour. Then rinse it thoroughly with hot water and dry. Let both top and bottom air dry thoroughly.

Low-Fat Cooking in a Clay Pot

What does low-fat mean?

If you want to maintain or gradually reach your ideal weight, you'll succeed with the low-fat formula. Low-fat means no more than 30% of the calories you eat in a day should come from fat. The calories you need to feel full are supplied by rice, bread, pasta, vegetables, lean meat, and fish. So it's simply a matter of paying attention to fat.

A low-fat meal might consist of a 4–6 oz piece of meat with sauce accompanied by a side dish rich in carbohydrates and salad.

Thanks to its special properties, a clay pot can help you achieve this goal. It lets you prepare a healthy meal of carbohydrates and protein with little or no fat.

Invisible and visible fat

No more than 25–30% of your daily intake of calories should come from fat, including the fats hidden in many foods. These fats, which are part of the ingredients in prepared foods you buy, should not exceed 27–37 g, which is half the recommended amount of fat per day. If you buy low-fat products it should be easy to stay below the limit.

You can then consume the rest of your fat as spreads on bread and in cooking. The following rule of thumb makes it a cinch. Just think in terms of teaspoons:

1 tsp = approximately 5 g fat
1 tsp fat with breakfast
2–3 tsp with lunch
2–3 tsp with dinner

Keeping these guidelines in mind, don't forget that fat is also vital for healthy nutrition. The essential fatty acids and fat-soluble vitamins A and E in particular are hidden in vegetable fats. When you prepare a low-fat main dish in the clay pot, you still have leeway, for example, to dress your salad with extra virgin olive oil or have a dessert made of fruit, sour cream, and nuts. This also gives you all the vitamins you need.

Use less fat for cooking

Instead of cream or crème fraîche, use low-fat sour cream or full-fat yogurt (6% fat) to bind sauces and soups. If you stir either of these up with a little cornstarch and briefly bring it to a boil, it won't curdle and slightly thickens the sauce. "Light" condensed milk (3% fat) doesn't curdle and is a good alternative for desserts.

For hearty casserole crusts, combine grated Parmesan cheese (fat content of 30%) with an equal amount of breadcrumbs, mix with a lot of finely chopped herbs, and sprinkle on top. For more low-fat alternatives, see pages 58–59.

Fry meat in a nonstick pan using little or no oil. Don't pour the fat from the pan into the clay pot. In the case of chicken, whether whole or in pieces, remove the skin and fat ahead of time (see Tip on page 41).

Side Dishes

Basmati Rice

Serves 4: In a small baking dish that fits in the oven along- side the clay pot, combine 2 cups water, $1/2$ tsp salt, 1 cup basmati rice, and 1 bay leaf. Cover the pot with aluminum foil and cook for 1 hour beside the clay pot.

If you want, you can mix 3–4 tbs of chopped herbs, such as parsley, dill, chervil, and tarragon into the cooked rice.

Potatoes

Serves 4: Rinse 4 to 6 large Idaho potatoes, pierce each one 3 or 4 times with a fork, wrap them in foil while wet with a sprig of rosemary or thyme, and place them on the rack around the clay pot. Together with the clay pot, cook them for 45–60 minutes.

For many dishes, you can put the potatoes in the clay pot. To serve 4, peel 1 lb potatoes, cut them up if desired, and cook them with the dish.

You can also cook the potatoes simultaneously on a baking sheet. In this case, rinse potatoes, cut in half, sprinkle with chopped herbs, (rosemary, oregano, or thyme) and place on a greased baking sheet. Place below the clay pot and cook for 1 hour.

Baguette Seasoned with Herbs

Slice baguette every 1–2 inches, cutting only $3/4$ of the way through the bread. Between the slices, spread a thin layer of pesto or tomato paste and insert several herb leaves such as basil, parsley, or thyme. Wrap bread in aluminum foil and bake for 20 minutes. Or place the baguette next to the clay pot and let it heat up during the last 10 minutes.

Couscous

This is an ideal side dish for all vegetable and meat dishes made in a clay pot. Just before the cooking time is over, bring the amount of water specified on the package of couscous to a boil with a pinch of salt. Then stir in the appropriate amount of couscous and a $1/2$ tsp butter. Cover and let sit 3–5 minutes. Fluff with a fork prior to serving.

Vegetables, Appetizers, and Snacks

Bring the Mediterranean right into your own home! Ratatouille, fennel, or grape leaves will fill your house with a southern Mediterranean fragrance, and will taste wonderfully aromatic. With these delicious vegetable dishes and sophisticated tidbits, family and friends will find themselves transported to a picturesque villa without stepping outside your house.

Quick Recipes

Ratatouille

SERVES 4:

> 3 large beefsteak tomatoes |
  2 bell peppers | 2 medium zucchini |
  1 eggplant | 1 large onion |
  2 cloves garlic | 1 tbs chopped thyme |
  2 tbs olive oil | 1/3 cup vegetable stock |
  Salt, preferably sea or kosher |
  Finely ground black pepper

1 | Rinse vegetables, clean, and slice. Peel and slice garlic. Arrange in the pre-soaked clay pot in alternating layers.

2 | Sprinkle each layer sparingly with salt, pepper, and thyme and drizzle the whole thing with olive oil and stock. Cover and bake in the oven at 475°F for 30 minutes.

Tomatoes and Haricot Vert

SERVES 4:

> 1 lb fresh haricot vert (small, French green beans) |
  1 can whole, peeled tomatoes (1 lb) |
  1 onion | 2 sage leaves |
  1 tsp olive oil | 1 pinch sugar |
  Salt, preferably sea or kosher |
  Finely ground black pepper

1 | Rinse beans, clean, and place in 1 quart boiling, salted water for 2–3 minutes. Remove from water, rinse with cold water, drain, and cut into pieces. Crush tomatoes and combine with tomato juice and beans in the pre-soaked clay pot.

2 | Peel and chop onion. Combine onion, sage, oil, salt, pepper, and sugar, add to the clay pot, and stir together. Cover and bake in the oven at 400°F for 45 minutes.

11

Also Good Cold
Fennel Niçoise

SERVES 4:

- 3 tomatoes
  1³/₄ lbs fennel
  1 clove garlic
  1 tsp fresh thyme
  ¼ tsp coriander seeds
  2 tbs raisins
  ²/₃ cup white wine
  1 tbs olive oil
  Salt, preferably sea
  or kosher
  Finely ground black pepper

- Prep time: 20 minutes
- Cooking time: 45 minutes
- Per serving approx:
  115 calories
- 5 g protein / 3 g fat /
  11 g carbohydrates

1 | Pour boiling water over tomatoes, peel, remove cores, and dice. Rinse fennel, clean, slice thinly, and place in the pre-soaked clay pot. Peel and dice garlic.

2 | Chop thyme, crush coriander seeds, and distribute both over the fennel along with garlic and raisins. Combine wine, oil,

salt, and pepper, pour over fennel, and top with tomatoes.

3 | Cover and braise vegetables in the oven at 400°F for 45 minutes.

Mediterranean
Sophisticated
Spicy Vegetable Ragout

SERVES 4:

- 6–8 shallots
  2 cloves garlic
  2 eggplant
  2 zucchini
  2 Idaho potatoes
  ½ tbs olive oil
  4 tomatoes
  2 red chili peppers
  6 pitted green olives
  1 tbs wine vinegar
  Salt, preferably sea
  or kosher
  Finely ground black pepper

- Prep time: 25 minutes
- Cooking time: 45 minutes
- Per serving approx:
  110 calories
- 4 g protein / 3 g fat /
  16 g carbohydrates

1 | Peel shallots and garlic and cut into quarters. Rinse eggplant and zucchini, clean, and cut into ½-inch cubes. Peel potatoes and cut into ½-inch cubes. In a large nonstick pan, heat oil and brown vegetables for 5 minutes. Season generously with salt and pepper and place in the pre-soaked clay pot.

2 | In the meantime, pour boiling water over tomatoes, peel, remove cores, and dice. Remove stems and seeds from chili peppers and cut into rings. Cut olives in half.

3 | Add all these ingredients and vinegar to vegetables, cover, and braise ragout in the oven at 425°F for 30 minutes. Remove cover and continue cooking vegetables for 15 minutes. Before serving, season to taste.

- Variation: This ragout is especially tasty with feta sprinkled on top.

Easy | Hearty

Potatoes Topped with Tuna

Serves 4:

- 6 large red potatoes
  1 (6-oz) can tuna packed in water
  2 tbs sour cream
  2 tbs low-fat milk
  2 tbs lemon juice
  3 lbs chopped parsley
  $1/2$ tsp fennel seeds
  1 tbs olive oil
  3 tbs freshly grated Parmesan
  Salt, preferably sea or kosher
  Finely ground black pepper

- Prep time: 20 minutes
- Cooking time: 45 minutes
- Per serving approx: 195 calories
- 13 g protein / 6 g fat / 21 g carbohydrates

1 | Peel potatoes and cut into slices about $1/2$ inch thick. Drain tuna and place in a bowl with sour cream and milk.

2 | Add lemon juice, $1/2$ tsp salt, pepper, parsley, and fennel seeds. Mix tuna with a fork to form a paste. Spread a little paste on all the potato slices and arrange side by side in the pre-soaked clay pot.

3 | Drizzle oil over potatoes and sprinkle with cheese. Cover and bake in the oven at 400°F for 35 minutes. Remove cover and bake for another 10 minutes.

Vegetarian
Mediterranean

Stuffed Pasta Shells

SERVES 4:

- 9 oz conchiglioni (large shells)
  1 lb spinach
  1 onion
  $1/2$ tbs olive oil
  $3/4$ cup feta
  2 tbs chopped parsley
  1 small egg
  $12/3$ cups vegetable stock
  $1/2$ cup freshly grated Swiss cheese
  Salt, preferably sea or kosher
  Finely ground black pepper

- Prep time: 30 minutes
- Cooking time: 50 minutes
- Per serving approx: 410 calories
- 19 g protein / 14 g fat / 52 g carbohydrates

1 | Soak pasta for 15–20 minutes in warm water. Rinse spinach thoroughly and drain.

2 | In the meantime, peel and chop onion. In a nonstick pan, heat oil and sauté onion until translucent. Stir in spinach and heat uncovered until liquid has evaporated. Chop spinach and season to taste with salt and pepper.

3 | Drain pasta. Crumble feta. Stir parsley, egg, and feta into spinach and fill pasta with mixture. Place pasta in the pre-soaked clay pot with the opening of the shell facing up. Pour stock over the top.

4 | Cover pasta and cook in the oven at 400°F for 40 minutes. Sprinkle with Swiss cheese and bake, uncovered, for another 10 minutes.

Photo left: **Stuffed Pasta Shells**   *Photo right:* **Potatoes Topped with Tuna** ➤

Takes More Time | For Company

Grape Leaves Stuffed with Rice and Pistachios

SERVES 4:

➤ ²/₃ cup round-grain rice

3 tomatoes

8–10 white mushrooms

2 cloves garlic

1¹/₂ tbs olive oil

3 tbs chopped parsley

2 tbs chopped pistachios

¹/₄ tsp ground coriander

12–16 marinated grape leaves

Salt, preferably sea or kosher

Finely ground black pepper

🕐 Prep time: 1 hour

🕐 Cooking time: 1 hour

➤ Per serving approx: 235 calories

➤ 9 g protein / 7 g fat / 32 g carbohydrates

1 | Place rice in a fine strainer, rinse thoroughly under cold water, drain, and pour into a bowl. Pour boiling water over 1 tomato, peel, remove core, and chop finely.

2 | Clean mushrooms and dice finely. Peel garlic. Heat ¹/₂ tbs olive oil over medium-high heat. Squeeze garlic through a press and add to oil. Add mushrooms and brown for 3 minutes.

3 | Combine parsley, tomato, mushrooms, pistachios, and rice and season with salt, pepper, and coriander.

4 | Rinse off grape leaves and spread out with the smooth side up. Cut off stems.

5 | Place 1–2 tsps filling on each leaf. Fold bottom and sides of leaves over the filling and roll up leaf.

6 | Rinse remaining tomatoes, cut in half, remove cores, and slice. In the pre-soaked clay pot, arrange alternating layers of grape leaf rolls and tomato slices. Whisk together 1¹/₂ cups water and remaining olive oil and pour over grape leaves. Cover and cook in the oven at 350°F for 1 hour.

> **1 Prepare grape leaves**
>
> *Spread out leaves with the smooth side up and cut off stems.*

> **2 Stuff grape leaves**
>
> *Place filling on the stem end of the leaf and fold the other sides over it.*

> **3 Wrap grape leaves**
>
> *Roll up leaves toward the tips and place in clay pot.*

17

Hearty | For Company

Savoy Cabbage au Gratin

SERVES 4:

- $1/4$ cup dried porcini mushrooms
- 1 small head Savoy cabbage ($1/4$ lbs)
- 1 onion
- 2 oz lean bacon
- $1/4$ cup vegetable stock
- 1 teaspoon marjoram
- Salt, preferably sea or kosher
- Finely ground black pepper
- 6 slices baguette
- $1/2$ cup milk
- $1/4$ cup Swiss cheese
- $1/2$ cups rice as side dish (see page 9)

🕐 Prep time: 35 minutes

🕐 Cooking time: 1 hour

➤ Per serving approx: 440 calories

➤ 17 g protein / 11 g fat / 67 g carbohydrates

1 | Soak mushrooms in $1/4$ cup warm water. Clean cabbage, rinse, and cut into strips. Peel onion. Dice onion and bacon.

2 | In a nonstick pan, fry bacon without fat. Add onion and sauté until translucent. Add cabbage, mushrooms with their soaking water, and stock, and braise over medium heat for 2–3 minutes. Season to taste with salt, pepper, and marjoram and place in the pre-soaked clay pot.

3 | Cover and cook in the oven at 400°F for 40 minutes. Place bread on top of vegetables. Drizzle with milk, sprinkle with cheese, and bake, uncovered, for 20 minutes.

Fruity | For Company

Baked Apples in Thyme Sauce

SERVES 4:

- 4 large tart apples
- 1 thin leek
- 1 clove garlic
- 2 oz smoked turkey breast
- $1/2$ stale roll of bread
- 3 tbs low-fat milk
- 2 tbs chopped parsley
- $1/2$ cup apple juice
- 2 oz fresh mozzarella
- 1 stalk thyme
- 1 tsp crème fraîche
- Salt, preferably sea or kosher
- Finely ground black pepper

🕐 Prep time: 25 minutes

🕐 Cooking time: 40 minutes

➤ Per serving approx: 155 calories

➤ 8 g protein / 4 g fat / 21 g carbohydrates

1 | Rinse apples and remove core from top. Enlarge the hole a little. Cut leek in half lengthwise, rinse well, and then cut white part into strips. Peel garlic and chop. Dice turkey finely. Soak roll in water, squeeze out, and crumble.

2 | Combine leek, garlic, turkey, bread, milk, and parsley, season with salt and pepper, then use to fill apples. Place apples in the pre-soaked clay pot. Pour apple juice over the top. Cover and bake in the oven at 425°F for 30 minutes.

3 | Dice mozzarella, place on apples, and bake, uncovered, for 10 minutes.

4 | Chop thyme. Place apples on prewarmed plates. Pour juice from clay pot into a small pot. Stir in crème fraîche and bring to a boil. Season with thyme, 1 pinch salt, and 1 pinch pepper and serve with apples.

Soups, Stews, and Casseroles

Don't you just love everything that comes out of a pot? Soups to warm the heart and soul, and satisfying stews and casseroles. Cooking these types of dishes in a clay pot has the added benefit of intensifying aromas and flavors. The results—from Lentil Soup with Mint to hearty Chicken Soup—are light and healthy, yet flavorful and delicious.

Quick Recipes

Tomato Rice Soup

SERVES 4:

➤ 12–14 firm, ripe tomatoes on the vine |
1 medium onion | 1 tbs olive oil |
1 $^2/_3$ cups vegetable stock |
$^1/_4$ cup round-grain rice |
$^1/_2$ tsp ground anise |
2 tbs chopped parsley |
Salt, preferably sea or kosher |
Finely ground black pepper

1 | Rinse tomatoes, dice finely, and place in pre-soaked clay pot. Peel onion and grate using a vegetable grater into the clay pot. Stir in oil, stock, rice, and anise.

2 | Cover soup and cook in the oven at 425°F for 40 minutes, stirring once. Season to taste with salt and pepper. Stir in parsley before serving.

Lentil Soup with Mint

SERVES 4:

➤ 1$^1/_2$ cups yellow lentils |
2 medium carrots | 2 stalks celery |
1 onion | 1$^1/_2$ quarts vegetable stock |
1 tbs olive oil | 1 tbs chopped mint |
Salt, preferably sea or kosher |
Finely ground black pepper

1 | Place lentils in a fine strainer and rinse under cold water. Peel and dice vegetables. Place everything in the pre-soaked clay pot and stir in stock and oil.

2 | Cover soup and cook in the oven (bottom rack) at 400°F for 50 minutes, stirring once. When done, purée soup in blender, season to taste with salt and pepper, and sprinkle with mint.

21

Asian | For Company

Chicken Stew

SERVES 4:

➤ **9 oz chicken breast**
  4 scallions
  1 head Chinese cabbage
  2 carrots
  1 chestnut-sized piece of fresh ginger
  1 tbs sunflower oil
  1½ quarts vegetable stock
  Light soy sauce
  4 oz Chinese egg noodles
  1¼ cups bean sprouts

🕑 Prep time: 30 minutes
🕑 Cooking time: 50 minutes
➤ Per serving approx: 445 calories
➤ 37 g protein / 16 g fat / 34 g carbohydrates

1 | Cut chicken into strips. Clean scallions, rinse, and cut into thin rings. Rinse cabbage and cut into strips. Peel and dice carrots. Peel and chop ginger.

2 | In a nonstick pan, heat oil and brown chicken breast over medium heat. Transfer to the pre-soaked clay pot. In the leftover oil, brown vegetables and transfer to clay pot. Stir in stock and 3–4 tbs soy sauce.

3 | Cover stew and cook in the oven at 400°F for 30 minutes. Stir in noodles and bean sprouts and cook stew for another 20 minutes. Season to taste with soy sauce.

Hearty | Easy

Vegetable Noodle Stew

SERVES 4:

➤ **4 oz smoked bacon**
  2 cloves garlic
  4 stalks celery
  2 carrots
  1 head broccoli
  ¼ head green cabbage
  4 tbs chopped parsley
  7 oz wagon wheel noodles
  4 tbs freshly grated pecorino
  Salt, preferably sea or kosher
  Finely ground black pepper

🕑 Prep time: 35 minutes
🕑 Cooking time: 50 minutes
➤ Per serving approx: 485 calories
➤ 23 g protein / 15 g fat / 64 g carbohydrates

1 | Dice bacon finely. Peel and chop garlic. Rinse vegetables, clean or peel as necessary, and cut into bite-size pieces. In a nonstick pan, brown bacon. Add garlic and vegetables and sauté for 2 minutes.

2 | Place everything in the pre-soaked clay pot. Pour in 1½ cups hot water. Season with 1 tsp salt and lots of pepper. Cover stew and cook in the oven at 400°F for 30 minutes.

3 | Stir parsley and noodles into soup and cook for another 20 minutes. Season stew to taste, transfer to bowls, and sprinkle cheese over each serving.

Photo top: **Vegetable Noodle Stew**   *Photo bottom:* **Chicken Stew** ➤

Vegetarian
Inexpensive

Noodle Casserole

SERVES 4:

- 3 large green bell peppers
  1 bunch scallions
  2 cloves garlic
  2 (14½-oz) cans whole peeled tomatoes
  1 tbs olive oil
  ½ bunch basil
  ¾ cup feta
  9 oz fettucine noodles
  Salt, preferably sea or kosher
  Finely ground black pepper

- Prep time: 40 minutes
- Cooking time: 50 minutes
- Per serving approx: 460 calories
- 15 g protein / 9 g fat / 56 g carbohydrates

1 | Clean bell peppers, rinse, and cut into wide strips. Clean scallions, rinse, and chop. Peel and chop garlic. Purée tomatoes with juice and season with salt and pepper.

2 | In a large nonstick pan, heat olive oil and sauté bell peppers, onions, and garlic for 4–5 minutes. Season with salt and pepper. Pick off basil leaves. Mash feta with a fork.

3 | In the pre-soaked clay pot, distribute vegetable mixture, noodles, ½ cup feta, tomato sauce, and basil. Sprinkle remaining cheese on top, close clay pot, and cook in the oven at 400°F for 50 minutes.

Hearty | Easy

Leek Lasagna with Chorizo

SERVES 4:

- 7 oz lasagna noodles
  1½ tbs butter
  2½ tbs flour
  2 cups low-fat milk
  1 pinch nutmeg
  6 large tomatoes
  2 thin leeks
  3 oz chorizo
  2 oz freshly grated Parmesan
  Salt, preferably sea or kosher
  Finely ground black pepper

- Prep time: 40 minutes
- Cooking time: 1 hour
- Per serving approx: 505 calories
- 23 g protein / 18 g fat / 61 g carbohydrates

1 | Soak noodles in cold water for 15 minutes and drain. In a pot, melt butter, stir in flour, and sauté over low heat without browning. Gradually stir in milk, simmer for 2 minutes, and season to taste with salt, pepper, and nutmeg.

2 | Pour boiling water over tomatoes, peel, and remove cores. Cut tomatoes crosswise into thin slices. Cut leek lengthwise and rinse well, then slice white part into narrow strips. Peel chorizo and slice thinly.

3 | In a nonstick pan without fat, fry leek and sausage over medium heat for 5 minutes. Remove, leaving sausage fat in the pan.

4 | In the pre-soaked clay pot, arrange alternating layers of a few lasagna noodles, a little of the milk sauce, leek, chorizo, and tomatoes, finishing with a layer of noodles. Cover this top layer well with sauce and sprinkle with cheese. Cover lasagna and cook in the oven at 400°F for 50 minutes. Remove cover and cook for another 10 minutes.

Photo top: **Noodle Casserole**   *Photo bottom:* **Leek Lasagna with Chorizo**

Easy

Eggplant Casserole

SERVES 4:

- 2 eggplant
  4 large red potatoes
  1 tbs olive oil
  2 (14½-oz) cans whole peeled tomatoes
  2 cloves garlic
  2 banana peppers
  1 (4-oz) ball mozzarella
  Salt, preferably sea or kosher
  Finely ground black pepper

- Prep time: 40 minutes
- Cooking time: 1 hour
- Per serving approx: 250 calories
- 13 g protein / 8 g fat / 30 g carbohydrates

1 | Blanch eggplant in lightly salted water for 3 minutes and then cut into ½-inch slices. Peel potatoes and slice ¼ inch thick. Brush potato and eggplant slices lightly with oil.

2 | Chop canned tomatoes finely without the juice (use for another recipe). Peel garlic, squeeze through a press, and add. Season with 1 tsp salt and a lot of pepper. Cut peppers in half, clean, and cut into quarters. Slice mozzarella in ¼-inch slices.

3 | In the pre-soaked clay pot, arrange alternating layers of eggplant and potatoes with a little of the tomato purée and peppers in between each layer. Pour remaining tomatoes over the top and cover with mozzarella. Cover casserole and cook in the oven (bottom rack) at 400°F for 1 hour.

Hearty

Vegetable and Lamb Stew

SERVES 4:

- 14 oz lean lamb
  8 shallots
  2 cloves garlic
  2 tbs olive oil
  2 medium carrots
  2 red bell peppers
  4 tomatoes
  1½ cups frozen peas
  2 stalks thyme
  2 cups vegetable stock
  Salt, preferably sea or kosher
  Finely ground black pepper

- Prep time: 40 minutes
- Cooking time: 1 hour
- Per serving approx: 390 calories
- 29 g protein / 11 g fat / 42 g carbohydrates

1 | Cut meat into 1-inch cubes. Peel shallots and garlic and cut into quarters. In a nonstick pan, heat oil until very hot and stir-fry meat, shallots, and garlic over medium heat for 3 minutes, then transfer to the pre-soaked clay pot.

2 | Peel carrots and slice. Cut bell peppers in half, clean, rinse, and cut into pieces. Pour boiling water over tomatoes, peel, remove cores, and dice. Rinse peas under hot water until thawed.

3 | Mix vegetables with meat in the clay pot. Place thyme stalks among them. Pour stock over the top. Cover dish and cook in the oven at 400°F for 1 hour. Season to taste with salt and pepper.

Photo top: Eggplant Casserole   *Photo bottom:* **Vegetable and Lamb Stew**

Hearty | Easy

Bulgur Casserole

SERVES 4:

- 2 cups bulgur

  1 onion

  12 white mushrooms

  4 oz cooked ham

  1/3 cup walnuts

  1 1/2 tbs butter

  2 cups tomato juice

  4 tbs chopped parsley

  2 oz freshly grated Edam cheese

  Salt, preferably sea or kosher

  Finely ground black pepper

- 🕐 Prep time: 30 minutes
- 🕐 Cooking time: 45 minutes
- ➤ Per serving approx: 405 calories
- ➤ 21 g protein / 10 g fat / 62 g carbohydrates

1 | Rinse bulgur under cold water and drain. Peel onion and dice. Clean mushrooms and slice. Dice ham. Chop walnuts coarsely.

2 | In a nonstick pan, heat butter and sauté onion, mushrooms, and ham over medium heat for 3 minutes. Season generously with salt and pepper. Transfer bulgur, tomato juice, and the contents of the pan to the pre-soaked clay pot and stir.

3 | Cover dish and cook in the oven at 400°F for 20 minutes. Stir mixture once more and cook for another 15 minutes. Combine parsley, walnuts, and cheese, sprinkle over bulgur, and cook for another 10 minutes.

Can Prepare in Advance

Brussels Sprout Casserole

SERVES 4:

- 1 lb Brussels sprouts

  4 small red potatoes

  5 oz bratwurst

  1 egg

  3 oz sour cream

  1 tbs (in total) chopped basil, thyme, and parsley

  1/3 cup milk

  1 tbs freshly grated Parmesan

  1 tbs breadcrumbs

  Salt, preferably sea or kosher

  Finely ground black pepper

- 🕐 Prep time: 30 minutes
- 🕐 Cooking time: 1 hour
- ➤ Per serving approx: 370 calories
- ➤ 19 g protein / 14 g fat / 41 g carbohydrates

1 | Clean Brussels sprouts, rinse, and blanch for 4 minutes in lightly salted boiling water. Remove with a slotted spoon and save water. Cut sprouts in half. Peel potatoes and slice into 1/4-inch discs.

2 | In the pre-soaked clay pot, arrange alternating layers of Brussels sprouts and potatoes. Peel sausage from its skin to make meatballs and incorporate in the layers. Pour in 1 cup Brussels sprout stock. Season with salt and pepper. Cover dish and cook in the oven at 400°F for 40 minutes.

3 | Whisk together egg, sour cream, herbs, milk, 1 pinch salt, and pepper and pour over the casserole. Combine Parmesan and breadcrumbs, sprinkle over the top, and bake uncovered for 20 minutes.

Photo left: **Brussels Sprout Casserole**   *Photo right:* **Bulgur Casserole** ➤

Meat, Poultry, and Game

If you think appetizing meat dishes require a lot of work both to prepare and to clean up the mess afterward, then you have not met the clay pot! It keeps the oven clean and you no longer have to maintain a constant vigil. Everything cooks up gently, turns out tender, and forms an enviable crust when you remove the cover during the last few minutes. Meat made easy—who could resist?

Quick Recipes

Honey-Crusted Turkey

SERVES 6:

➤ 2 lbs turkey thigh | Ground coriander |
8 shallots | 2 large quinces | $^2/_3$ cup dry
white wine | $^2/_3$ cup vegetable stock |
2 tsp yellow mustard seeds |
3 tbs honey | Salt, preferably sea
or kosher | Finely ground black pepper

1 | Rub salt, pepper, and coriander into meat
and place in the pre-soaked clay pot. Peel
shallots and cut in half. Scrape quinces, cut
into pieces, and add quinces and shallots
to the clay pot. Pour in wine and stock.

2 | Cover meat and cook in the oven
(bottom rack) at 400°F for 45 minutes.
Crush mustard seeds coarsely, combine with
honey and pepper, and brush onto meat.
Cook, uncovered, for another 15 minutes.

Bell Pepper Pork Cutlets

SERVES 4:

➤ 4 pork cutlets | 2 tbs pesto | 2 bell
peppers | 2 tomatoes | 4 sun-dried
tomatoes | 4 pitted green olives |
$^1/_2$ cup dry white wine | 1 tbs olive oil |
$1^1/_2$ lbs potatoes as side dish (see
page 9) | Salt, preferably sea or kosher

1 | Slice cutlets in half and spread with
pesto. Rinse and clean vegetables. Cut
bell peppers into strips and slice fresh
tomatoes. Chop dried tomatoes and
cut olives in half.

2 | Layer cutlets and vegetables in the
pre-soaked clay pot with sun-dried
tomatoes and olives in between. Whisk
together wine, oil, and 1 pinch salt and
pour over the top. Cover and cook in
the oven at 400°F for 40 minutes.

Hearty | For Company

Olive-Crusted Lamb Loin

SERVES 6:

- 1¾ lbs lamb loin
- 2 cloves garlic
- 1 tbs black olive paste (or tapenade)
- 2 tbs olive oil
- 2 scallions
- 4 tomatoes
- 1 lb green beans
- ⅓ cup red wine
- 4 stalks thyme
- ⅓ cup feta
- 2 lbs potatoes as side dish (see page 9)
- Salt, preferably sea or kosher
- Finely ground black pepper

🕐 Prep time: 35 minutes
🕐 Cooking time: 1 hour 30 minutes

- Per serving approx: 365 calories
- 29 g protein / 13 g fat / 35 g carbohydrates

1 | Soak clay pot and place lamb loin inside. Pierce lamb with the tip of a kitchen knife about 6 times in well-spaced locations. Peel garlic. Cut 1 clove into matchsticks and place them inside the holes in the lamb. Combine olive paste and 1 tbs olive oil and brush onto lamb.

2 | Clean scallions, rinse, and cut into pieces. Chop remaining garlic clove. Pour boiling water over tomatoes, peel, remove cores, and dice.

Rinse beans, clean, and cut into pieces.

3 | Distribute vegetables and garlic around the lamb. Season everything lightly with salt and pepper. Pour in red wine. Distribute remaining olive oil and thyme sprigs over the meat and vegetables.

4 | Close the pot and cook in the oven (bottom rack) at 425°F for 30 minutes. Then move to the center rack and cook at 350°F for 1 hour. Ten minutes before it's done, crumble feta and sprinkle over meat.

> 1 **Pierce meat**
> *Pierce lamb loin with the tip of a kitchen knife.*

> 2 **Stud with garlic**
> *Press garlic matchsticks deep into the holes.*

> 3 **Mash cheese**
> *Finely mash cheese with a fork and sprinkle on top.*

33

For Special Occasions

Pork Tenderloin with Artichokes

SERVES 4:

- 1 pork tenderloin
  4 sprigs rosemary
  2 tbs Dijon mustard
  $1/2$ lemon
  4 carrots
  10–12 pearl onions
  2 large artichokes
  1 cup vegetable stock
  $1/2$ cup yogurt, drained of all liquid
  Salt, preferably sea or kosher
  Finely ground black pepper

- Prep time: 35 minutes
- Cooking time: 2 hours
- Per serving approx: 303 calories
- 47 g protein / 8 g fat / 8 g carbohydrates

1 | Rub salt and pepper into meat and place in the pre-soaked clay pot. Place rosemary sprigs around pork. Squeeze lemon juice into mustard, whisk together briefly, and brush meat with mustard.

2 | Peel carrots and slice diagonally. Peel onions.

Remove stems from artichokes and break off coarse, outermost leaves. Pare down with a knife. Cut off tips. Scrape out the choke (fuzzy center) with a spoon, rinse artichokes, and cut into eighths.

3 | Arrange vegetables all around the roast and pour stock over the top. Cover dish and roast in the oven (bottom rack) at 425°F for 30 minutes. Reduce heat to 350°F and roast for another 1 hour and 30 minutes.

4 | Remove roast from the pot and keep meat warm. Stir yogurt into vegetables. Season to taste with salt and pepper and serve with roast.

Hearty

Sauerbraten with Pine Nuts

SERVES 4:

- $1^3/4$ lbs marinated sauerbraten
  2 onions
  2 tbs sunflower oil
  $2/3$ cup raisins
  $2/3$ cup dry red wine
  2 bay leaves
  1 slice dark pumpernickel

1 tbs apple butter
$1/3$ cup pine nuts
Salt, preferably sea or kosher
Finely ground black pepper

- Prep time: 30 minutes
- Cooking time: 1 hour 30 minutes
- Per serving approx: 436 calories
- 47 g protein / 14 g fat / 28 g carbohydrates

1 | Remove sauerbraten from marinade and dry. Set aside marinade. Peel and dice onions. In a roasting pan, heat oil until very hot and brown meat on all sides, then transfer to the pre-soaked clay pot.

2 | Brown onions and raisins in leftover oil and add to meat. Add red wine, marinade, bay leaves, salt, and pepper. Cover roast and cook in the oven (bottom rack) at 400°F for 1 hour.

3 | Crumble bread finely and stir into sauce along with apple butter. Season sauce to taste and cook for another 30 minutes. Toast pine nuts in a dry pan without fat, sprinkle over the top, and serve.

Photo top: **Sauerbraten with Pine Nuts** *Photo bottom:* **Pork Tenderloin with Artichokes**

Can Prepare in Advance

Pot au feu with Vegetables

SERVES 6:

- ➤ 14 oz lean pork roast
- 14 oz veal roast
- 2 onions
- 2 cloves garlic
- 1½ tbs butter
- 3 bay leaves
- 3 carrots
- 3 small white turnips
- 10–12 marinated cocktail onions
- 2 cups light-colored beer
- Salt, preferably sea or kosher
- Finely ground black pepper

- ⏱ Prep time: 20 minutes
- ⏱ Cooking time: 1 hour 30 minutes
- ➤ Per serving approx: 305 calories
- ➤ 45 g protein / 7 g fat / 8 g carbohydrates

1 | Cut each roast into quarters and rub with salt and pepper. Peel onions and garlic and dice finely. In a large nonstick pan, heat butter and brown meat on all sides over high heat, then transfer to the pre-soaked clay pot. Sauté onions and garlic in leftover fat until translucent and add to pot. Mix in bay leaves.

2 | Peel carrots and turnips and cut into quarters. Add to meat along with drained cocktail onions. Sprinkle everything with salt and pepper. Pour in beer. Cover dish and cook in the oven (bottom rack) at 350°F for 1 hour and 30 minutes.

 TIP You can enhance this dish by adding green beans, leek, and herbs such as rosemary and thyme.

Easy | Exotic

Lamb Curry with Apples

SERVES 4:

- ➤ 1¼ lbs lean lamb (leg)
- 2 onions
- 2 cloves garlic
- 1 tsp ground ginger
- 1 tbs curry
- 1 tbs olive oil
- ½ cup dry white wine
- 3 tart apples
- 6 pitted prunes
- Salt, preferably sea or kosher
- Finely ground black pepper

- ⏱ Prep time: 30 minutes
- ⏱ Cooking time: 1 hour
- ➤ Per serving approx: 290 calories
- ➤ 32 g protein / 9 g fat / 17 g carbohydrates

1 | Remove fat from lamb and dice. Place meat in the pre-soaked clay pot. Peel onions and garlic, chop, and add. Season everything with ginger, curry, 1 tsp salt, and lots of pepper.

2 | Pour in oil, wine, and ½ cup water and mix everything together. Cover meat and cook in the oven at 400°F for 30 minutes.

3 | Peel apples and grate coarsely. Stir into meat along with prunes. Cover and cook for another 30 minutes. Then season to taste once more with salt and pepper.

 TIP You can also substitute turkey or chicken breast for the lamb.

Inexpensive
For Company

Spicy Provençal Chicken

SERVES 4:

- **4 chicken thighs and legs (8 pieces total)**
  2 cloves garlic
  3 tsp herbes de Provence
  1/2 tsp Hungarian hot paprika
  1 tbs olive oil
  2 tbs lemon juice
  1 oz lean bacon
  3 medium red potatoes
  1 tbs chopped lemon thyme
  2 tomatoes
  Salt, preferably sea or kosher
  Finely ground black pepper

- Marinating time: 1 hour
- Prep time: 30 minutes
- Cooking time: 1 hour
- Per serving approx: 270 calories
- 40 g protein / 4 g fat / 17 g carbohydrates

1 | Remove skin and fat from chicken pieces. Rinse and dry chicken. Peel garlic and squeeze through a press. Combine with herbs, paprika, salt, pepper, olive oil, and lemon juice. Brush onto meat and marinate for 1 hour.

2 | Dice bacon. Peel and dice potatoes and sprinkle with lemon thyme. Pour boiling water over tomatoes, peel, remove cores, and dice. Mix all these ingredients together, transfer to the pre-soaked clay pot, and sprinkle with salt and pepper.

3 | Place chicken pieces on top of potatoes and drizzle remaining marinade over the top. Cover dish and cook in the oven at 400°F for 1 hour.

Low-Cal
Can Prepare in Advance

Pork Ragout with Apricots

SERVES 4:

- **1 1/2 lbs pork (from the leg)**
  2 onions
  1 tbs butter
  1/2 cup tomato juice
  1/2 cup dry white wine
  1 tsp Hungarian sweet paprika
  2 bay leaves
  24 dried apricots
  Salt, preferably sea or kosher
  Finely ground black pepper

- Prep time: 35 minutes
- Cooking time: 1 hour
- Per serving approx: 295 calories
- 39 g protein / 8 g fat / 11 g carbohydrates

1 | Dice pork coarsely. Peel onions and dice finely.

2 | In a nonstick pan, heat butter until very hot, and sauté meat and onions over medium heat for 5 minutes. Sprinkle with salt and pepper and transfer to the pre-soaked clay pot. Combine tomato juice, wine, paprika, and a little salt and pepper and add to the clay pot. Add bay leaves.

3 | Cover and cook in the oven (bottom rack) at 400°F for 30 minutes. In the meantime, cut dried apricots in half and soak in water for 20 minutes.

4 | Add apricots to meat. Cover and cook for another 30 minutes.

Inexpensive | For Special Occasions

Stuffed Chicken with Vegetables

SERVES 4:

- ¼ cup basmati rice
  1 cleaned frying chicken (about 3 lbs)
  4 tomatoes
  ¼ cup currants
  ⅓ cup pine nuts
  1 pinch ground allspice
  1 tbs fresh chopped mint
  1 bunch scallions
  1 large red bell pepper
  2 zucchini
  ½ cup white wine
  2 tsp olive oil
  1 cup basmati rice as side dish
  Salt, preferably sea or kosher
  Finely ground black pepper

🕐 Prep time: 45 minutes
🕐 Cooking time: 1 hour 30 minutes

- Per serving approx: 465 calories
- 41 g protein / 12 g fat / 44 g carbohydrates

1 | Cover rice with water and soak for 30 minutes. Rinse chicken inside and out, pat dry, and remove as much fat as possible (see Tip and below). Rub with salt and pepper.

2 | Rinse tomatoes. Grate one on a fine vegetable grater.

3 | Drain rice. Mix with currants, pine nuts, grated tomato, ½ tsp salt, ½ tsp black pepper, allspice, and mint and stuff into chicken. Close opening. Place chicken in the pre-soaked clay pot, cover, and roast in the oven at 425°F for 30 minutes.

4 | In the meantime, pour boiling water over remaining tomatoes, peel, remove cores, and dice. Rinse onions, bell pepper, and zucchini, clean, and cut into small pieces.

5 | Distribute vegetables around chicken, season everything lightly with salt and pepper, and drizzle with wine and olive oil. Cover and cook at 350°F for 1 hour. For last 10 minutes, bake uncovered to brown.

TIP

Removing chicken fat
The fat is mainly found on the thighs, neck, back, and rear of the breast.

1 Remove fat from chicken

Cut into skin in many places and remove fat from underneath.

2 Grate tomato

Grate firm tomatoes with the peel using a fine vegetable grater, just as you would potatoes.

3 Stuff chicken

Don't pack stuffing tightly because it swells during cooking.

4 Close chicken

Close opening using kitchen string or two metal skewers.

Low-Cal | Hearty

Rolled Turkey Roast over Sauerkraut

SERVES 4:

- 1 rolled turkey roast (1^3/$_4$ lbs)

  8 large slices prosciutto (about 6 oz)

  4 sun-dried tomatoes

  1 tbs pesto

  2 tbs freshly grated Parmesan

  1 tsp juniper berries

  3 bay leaves

  2^1/$_4$ cups sauerkraut

  1 cup hard cider

  1 tsp honey

  Salt, preferably sea or kosher

  Finely ground black pepper

- 🕐 Prep time: 40 minutes
- 🕐 Cooking time: 1 hour
- ➤ Per serving approx: 295 calories
- ➤ 41 g protein / 9 g fat / 16 g carbohydrates

1 | Unroll meat and top with 2 slices of prosciutto. Chop tomatoes, combine with pesto and Parmesan, and spread over prosciutto. Roll up meat and secure with kitchen string.

2 | Dice 3 slices prosciutto. Mix into sauerkraut along with juniper berries and 1 bay leaf and transfer to the pre-soaked clay pot. Stir together cider, honey, ^{1}/$_2$ tsp salt, and lots of pepper, and pour over the top.

3 | Place roast on top and cover with remaining bay leaf and prosciutto. Cover and cook in the oven (bottom rack) at 400°F for 1 hour.

Sophisticated | Low-Cal

Rabbit in Wine Sauce

SERVES 6:

- 1 cleaned rabbit (about 3 lbs) cut into 6 pieces

  2 shallots

  1 tbs olive oil

  3 bay leaves

  5 tbs chopped parsley

  1 cup dry white wine

  2 cloves garlic

  2 tbs yogurt (drained)

  10–12 threads saffron

  ^{1}/$_2$ tsp cornstarch

  Salt, preferably sea or kosher

  Finely ground black pepper

- 🕐 Prep time: 40 minutes
- 🕐 Cooking time: 1 hour 30 minutes

- ➤ Per serving approx: 695 calories
- ➤ 32 g protein / 12 g fat / 31 g carbohydrates

1 | Rub salt and pepper into rabbit pieces. Peel shallots and cut in half. In a nonstick pan, heat oil and brown rabbit and shallots on all sides over medium heat. Transfer to pre-soaked clay pot.

2 | Add bay leaf and 3 tbs parsley to clay pot. Combine wine, 1 cup water, and ^{1}/$_2$ tsp salt and pour ^{2}/$_3$ of this mixture over rabbit. Cover and cook in the oven at 425°F for 1 hour and 30 minutes.

3 | Peel garlic, squeeze through a press, and add to yogurt. Stir in saffron, cornstarch, and remaining wine until smooth.

4 | After cooking, place meat and shallots in a bowl. Add stock from the clay pot to the yogurt sauce and heat while stirring constantly until it becomes creamy. Season to taste, pour over rabbit, and sprinkle with remaining parsley.

Fish and Seafood

Fish—there's no getting enough of this healthy, delicious, and versatile food. The clay pot guarantees easy, healthy preparation and there's no lack of variety when you pair seafood with vegetables like fennel, Swiss chard, Savoy cabbage, and tomatoes. Here are eight fish and seafood recipes, more than enough for every day of the week!

Quick Recipes

Tuna and New Potatoes

SERVES 6:

➤ 2 bell peppers │ 5 tomatoes │ 5 medium
red potatoes │ 1 large onion │ 1 clove
garlic │ 1 tbs olive oil │ 1 tsp Hungarian
sweet paprika │ 1 cup dry white wine │
18 oz tuna cut into 1-inch slices │
Salt, preferably sea or kosher │
Finely ground black pepper

1 │ Rinse vegetables and clean or peel. Cut
bell peppers into strips. Dice tomatoes,
potatoes, and fish.

2 │ Dice onion and garlic and sauté in oil
until translucent. Add vegetables and fish
and sauté for 2 minutes. Season with salt,
pepper, and paprika. Transfer to the pre-
soaked clay pot along with the wine, cover,
and cook in the oven at 425°F for 40 minutes.

Rockfish with Fennel

SERVES 6:

➤ 2 small fennel bulbs │ 2 tomatoes │
12 mushrooms │ $1/2$ tsp olive oil │
2 large rockfish filets (14 oz each) │
2 tbs lemon juice │ 8 basil leaves │
4 tbs dry white wine (may substitute
vegetable stock) │ Salt, preferably sea
or kosher │ Finely ground black pepper

1 │ Rinse and clean vegetables. Wipe off
mushrooms. Slice all vegetables thinly.
Sauté in oil for 2–3 minutes. Season with
salt and pepper. Cut each rockfish filet
into 3 pieces, season, and drizzle with
lemon juice.

2 │ In the pre-soaked clay pot, layer
vegetables and fish with basil. Pour in
wine, cover, and cook in the oven at 400°F
for 40 minutes.

Easy | For Company

Red Snapper with Tomatoes

SERVES 4:

- 1 bunch scallions

  4 tomatoes

  1 lemon

  1 cleaned red snapper (about 2 lbs)

  2 sprigs rosemary

  1 tsp olive oil

  1/2 cup dry white wine

  3 tbs chopped parsley

  1 oz feta

  1 cup rice as side dish (see page 9)

  Salt, preferably sea or kosher

  Finely ground black pepper

- Prep time: 25 minutes
- Cooking time: 40 minutes
- Per serving approx: 410 calories
- 30 g protein / 12 g fat / 42 g carbohydrates

1 | Clean scallions, rinse, and cut into 1-inch pieces. Pour boiling water over tomatoes, peel, core, and cut into eighths. Cut lemon into 5 thin slices.

2 | Rub inside and outside of fish with salt and pepper.

Place 1 sprig rosemary and 2 lemon slices inside the cavity of the fish. Lay 3 lemon slices in the pre-soaked oval fish clay pot and place the fish on top.

3 | In a nonstick pan, heat oil and sauté vegetables with remaining rosemary over medium heat for 2–3 minutes. Stir in wine and parsley, bring to a boil, season with salt and pepper, and distribute over fish. Crumble cheese coarsely and sprinkle on top. Cover fish and cook in the oven at 400°F for 40 minutes.

Can Prepare in Advance

Cod with Swiss Chard

SERVES 4:

- 1 bunch Swiss chard

  18 oz cod fillet

  4 tbs chopped dill

  1 1/4 lbs red potatoes

  1 cup sour cream

  1 tsp cornstarch

  1/2 cup freshly grated Edam cheese

  Salt, preferably sea or kosher

  Finely ground black pepper

- Prep time: 35 minutes
- Cooking time: 40 minutes
- Per serving approx: 290 calories
- 32 g protein / 8 g fat / 21 g carbohydrates

1 | Clean chard, rinse, and cut into strips. Blanch for 3 minutes in lightly salted, boiling water. Place in the pre-soaked clay pot. Cut fish into strips 1 inch wide, distribute on top of chard, season with salt and pepper, and sprinkle with dill.

2 | Peel potatoes, slice and layer over fish in a scale pattern. Season with salt and pepper. Whisk together sour cream and cornstarch and spread over potatoes. Sprinkle with cheese.

3 | Cover dish and cook in the oven at 425°F for 40 minutes. Remove cover after 30 minutes.

Photo top: Red Snapper with Tomatoes   Photo bottom: Cod with Swiss Chard

For Company | Exotic
Calamari in Sherry

SERVES 4:

➤ 2¹/₄ lbs cleaned squid

5 shallots

2 tbs olive oil

1 tbs black peppercorns

3 bay leaves

1 level tsp sugar

¹/₄ cup semi-dry sherry

¹/₄ cup mild sherry vinegar

1 tsp chopped dill

1 tsp chopped parsley

Salt, preferably sea or kosher

🕐 Prep time: 30 minutes

🕐 Cooking time: 50 minutes

➤ Per serving approx: 290 calories

➤ 36 g protein / 8 g fat / 12 g carbohydrates

1 | Rinse squid and cut tubes into bite-size pieces. Peel shallots, cut in half, and then into strips.

2 | Pour olive oil into the pre-soaked clay pot, distribute shallots on top, and then squid. Sprinkle with pepper-corns, bay leaves, 1 level tsp salt, and sugar. Stir together.

3 | Cover and cook in the oven at 400°F for 20 minutes. Then reduce heat to 350°F and cook for another 20 minutes. Pour sherry and vinegar over calamari and cook for 10 minutes. Sprinkle with dill and parsley.

Low-Cal | For Company
Pot of Mussels

SERVES 4:

➤ 3 lbs mussels

2 onions

2 cloves garlic

2 stalks celery

1 tbs olive oil

2 (14¹/₂-oz) cans whole, peeled tomatoes

1 chili pepper

1 sprig rosemary

1 sprig thyme

1 cup dry white wine

4 slices baguette as side dish (see page 9)

Salt, preferably sea or kosher

Finely ground black pepper

🕐 Prep time: 40 minutes

🕐 Cooking time: 30 minutes

➤ Per serving approx: 265 calories

➤ 12 g protein / 7 g fat / 30 g carbohydrates

1 | Clean mussels (see Tip). Peel and slice onions and garlic. Rinse celery and cut into small pieces.

2 | In a pot, heat oil and saute vegetables for 3 minutes. Remove tomatoes from juice and chop. Add tomatoes, chili pepper, herbs, and wine to the vegetables. Simmer for 2 minutes, season with salt and pepper, and let cool.

3 | Rinse mussels several times, transfer to the large pre-soaked clay pot while dripping wet, and pour sauce over the top. Cover mussels and cook in the oven at 425°F for 30 minutes until they have all opened.

TIP
Cleaning mussels
Throw away mussels that are open before cooking. Also throw away mussels that stay closed after you have cooked them. In both cases, the mussels have gone bad.

Photo top: Pot of Mussels   *Photo bottom:* Calamari in Sherry ➤

Low-Cal | For Company
Arctic Char in Savoy Cabbage

SERVES 4:

➤ 4 dried morel mushrooms
1 head Savoy cabbage
1 tsp green peppercorns
$1/2$ cup cream cheese
2 tbs chopped parsley
2 skinless arctic char filets (about $1^1/4$ lbs)
$1/2$ cup fish stock
$1/2$ cup white wine
2 tbs crème fraîche
$1^3/4$ lbs potatoes as side dish (see page 9)
Salt, preferably sea or kosher
Finely ground black pepper

🕑 Soaking time: 1 hour
🕑 Prep time: 40 minutes
🕑 Cooking time: 45 minutes
➤ Per serving approx: 390 calories
➤ 41 g protein / 10 g fat / 30 g carbohydrates

1 | Soak morels in water for 1 hour, then remove and rinse. Remove 8 leaves of cabbage and pare the thick ribs with a knife until flat. Blanch for 4 minutes in boiling, salted water, rinse under cold water, and pat dry. Crush peppercorns slightly.

2 | Chop morels and combine half with cream cheese and parsley. Lightly salt fish fillets. Place 1 fillet on top of 4 over-lapped cabbage leaves, cover with mushroom paste, and fold leaves over the top. Repeat with the second fillet. Transfer to the pre-soaked clay pot. Stir together stock, wine, a little salt and pepper, and the remaining morels, and pour over fish.

3 | Cover fish and cook in the oven at 400°F for 45 minutes. Remove from oven and keep warm. Stir crème fraîche into stock.

Easy
Haddock Wrapped in Leek

SERVES 4:

➤ 2 lbs cleaned haddock
3 tbs lemon juice
1 thick leek
3 red potatoes
2 carrots
2 large shallots
1 cup fish stock
1 tsp fennel seeds
$1^1/2$ tsp softened butter
2 tbs chopped parsley
2 tbs chopped dill

2 tbs crème fraîche
Salt, preferably sea or kosher
Finely ground black pepper

🕑 Prep time: 30 minutes
🕑 Cooking time: 45 minutes
➤ Per serving approx: 350 calories
➤ 48 g protein / 10 g fat / 18 g carbohydrates

1 | Rub salt and pepper into fish and drizzle with lemon juice. Clean leek, cut open lengthwise, and rinse. Blanch for 5 minutes in boiling, salted water, rinse under cold water, and separate layers. Wrap fish in these leaves and transfer to the pre-soaked clay pot.

2 | Peel vegetables and cut into narrow strips. Place vegetables around the fish, season lightly with salt and pepper, pour in stock, and sprinkle with fennel seeds. Cover fish and cook in the oven at 400°F for 35 minutes.

3 | Knead together butter and herbs and distribute over fish. Cook fish in the oven for 10 minutes uncovered, remove, and keep warm. Stir crème fraîche into vegetables.

Desserts and Bread

The versatile clay pot can also be used to create delicious desserts and pastries. It's even marvelously suited to baking bread. Berry soufflé, apricot sticky buns, red wine peaches with ginger, olive bread, and nut bread; nothing is too much for the clay pot. Choose from among these delectable desserts and breads.

Quick Recipes

Apple Bread Pudding

SERVES 4:

➤ 3 tart apples | 6 slices dry white bread | $1/4$ cup low-fat milk | 3 tbs butter | 2 tsp cinnamon | $1/2$ cup brown sugar | $1/4$ cup maple syrup | $1/4$ cup cream

1 | Peel apples, quarter, and slice. Crumble bread and sprinkle part of it on the bottom of the pre-soaked clay pot, drizzle with milk, and top with butter cut into bits, cinnamon, sugar, and apples. Layer all the ingredients this way.

2 | Whisk together maple syrup and cream and drizzle over the top. Cover pudding and bake in the oven at 400°F for 50 minutes.

Berry Soufflé

SERVES 4:

➤ 2 medium eggs | 1 lb low-fat sour cream | $1/3$ cup low-fat milk | $3/4$ cup semolina | 10 tbs sugar | 1 tsp vanilla | 1 egg white | $1^1/4$ cups mixed berries | $1/4$ cup grated coconut

1 | Separate eggs. Combine sour cream, milk, egg yolks, semolina, 6 tbs sugar, and vanilla. Beat egg whites with 2 tbs of sugar until stiff. Fold half the egg whites and the berries into the sour cream and transfer to the pre-soaked clay pot.

2 | Mix remaining beaten egg whites with remaining sugar and grated coconut and spread on top. Cover and bake in the oven at 425°F for 30 minutes, then remove cover and bake for another 10 minutes.

Traditional | Easy

Apricot Sticky Buns

SERVES 4:

➤ 3½ tbs butter
4 fresh apricots (see Tip)
1 cinnamon stick
1 thin piece lemon peel
6 tbs sugar
2 cups flour
1 packet yeast (1½ tsp)
½ cup lukewarm water
⅓ cup almonds
3 tbs powdered sugar
Salt

⏱ Prep time: 45 minutes
⏱ Cooking time: 50 minutes
➤ Per serving approx:
595 calories
➤ 13 g protein / 18 g fat /
95 g carbohydrates

1 | Melt butter. Rinse apricots, cut in half, and remove pits. In the pre-soaked clay pot, mix apricots with cinnamon, lemon peel, and 3 tbs sugar and let stand.

2 | Sift flour with a pinch of salt into a bowl. Stir yeast and remaining sugar into water and pour over flour along with melted butter. Work

mix with a dough hook for 5 minutes. Cover and let rise in a warm place for 30 minutes.

3 | At the same time, cover apricots and precook in the oven at 400°F for 20 minutes, then remove from oven. Chop almonds.

4 | Knead dough. Shape into dough balls slightly larger than walnuts, arrange on top of apricots, and sprinkle with almonds. Cover sticky buns and cook in the oven at 400°F for 30 minutes. Sprinkle with powdered sugar and caramelize under the broiler or at 475°F for 2–3 minutes.

TIP

Apricots
Instead of fresh apricots, you can also use 8 dried. Cut in half and soak, then drain.

Recipe from Spain

Red Wine Peaches with Ginger

SERVES 4:

➤ 4 large peaches
½-inch piece fresh ginger
1 cinnamon stick
2 whole cloves
3½ tbs sugar
3 cups dry red wine
2 tsp brown sugar

⏱ Prep time: 25 minutes
⏱ Cooking time: 30 minutes
➤ Per serving approx:
250 calories
➤ 1 g protein / 1 g fat /
31 g carbohydrates

1 | Pour boiling water over peaches and peel. Place whole peaches in the pre-soaked clay pot. Peel ginger, chop, and sprinkle on top along with spices and sugar. Add red wine. Cover and bake in the oven at 400°F for 30 minutes, turning after 15 minutes.

2 | Sprinkle each peach with ½ tsp brown sugar and caramelize under the broiler or at 475°F for 2–3 minutes. Let fruit cool in the wine.

Mediterranean
For Company

Olive Bread

MAKES 1 LOAF IN THE
SMALL CLAY POT:

➤ 2$^1/_2$ cups all purpose flour
  1 cup whole-wheat flour
  2 packets yeast (3 tsp)
  1 tsp sugar
  1 tbs olive oil
  6-8 pitted black olives
  1 tbs dried thyme
  1 tbs milk
  Flour for working dough
  Olive oil for greasing
  clay pot
  1 tsp salt

🕐 Prep time: 30 minutes
🕐 Rising time: 1 hour
  30 minutes
🕐 Baking time: 1 hour
➤ Per slice (10 slices) approx:
  175 calories
➤ 5 g protein / 5 g fat /
  29 g carbohydrates

1 | Combine flours and salt.
Stir yeast and sugar into
1 cup lukewarm water until
smooth. Gradually stir water
and 1 tbs olive oil into flour.
Knead to form a very soft
dough. Knead vigorously for
5 minutes, shape into a ball,
cover, and let rise for 1 hour
in a warm place. Chop olives
roughly.

2 | Knead dough again, pull
apart, sprinkle with olives,
and work olives into the
dough. Shape dough into
an oval. Lightly oil the pre-
soaked clay pot, sprinkle
with thyme, and place bread
inside. Brush loaf with milk,
cover, and let rise for another
30 minutes.

3 | Bake bread in the oven
(bottom rack) at 400°F for
1 hour, removing cover
during the last 10 minutes.

Recipe from France

Nut Bread

MAKES 1 LOAF IN THE
SMALL CLAY POT:

➤ 3 cups whole wheat flour
  2 packets yeast (3 tsp)
  $^1/_2$ tsp sugar
  1 tsp fine sea salt
  $^1/_2$ cup walnuts
  1 tbs milk
  Flour for kneading
  Oil for greasing clay pot

🕐 Prep time: 30 minutes
🕐 Rising time: 1 hour
🕐 Baking time: 1 hour
➤ Per slice (10 slices) approx:
  170 calories
➤ 7 g protein / 4 g fat /
  26 g carbohydrates

1 | Sift flour into a bowl and
form a well in the center.
Stir yeast and sugar into
$^1/_4$ cup lukewarm water
until smooth, pour into well,
and mix with part of flour.
Sprinkle salt on top, stir in
$^3/_4$ cup water to form a soft
dough, and then knead.

2 | Cover dough and let rise
for 30 minutes in a warm
place. Knead again and pull
apart. Chop walnuts coarsely
and distribute on top. Fold
dough together and continue
kneading until walnuts are
evenly distributed.

3 | Shape dough into a roll.
Brush the pre-soaked clay pot
with oil and place roll inside.
Brush surface of loaf with
milk. Cover dough and let
rise for another 30 minutes.

4 | Bake bread in the oven
(bottom rack) at 400°F for
1 hour, removing cover
during the last 10 minutes.

Photo top: **Olive Bread**   Photo bottom: **Nut Bread** ➤

Hidden Fat and Some Alternatives

Learn about hidden sources of fat. This table provides you with suggestions for replacing high-fat products.

High-Fat Food	Fat Content in g*	Low-Fat Food	Fat Content in g*
Dairy products		**Dairy products**	
Crème fraîche	40	Sour cream	10
Yogurt (3.5% fat)	3.5	Low-fat yogurt	1.5
Cream (30% fat)	30	Condensed milk (4%) or sour cream + cornstarch	4
Sour cream	10	Condensed milk (4%)	4
Whole milk	3.5	Low-fat milk	1.5
Cheese		**Cheese**	
Camembert	22	Low-fat Camembert	13
Edam/Gouda/Swiss	Approx. 30	Low-fat Edam/Gouda/Swiss	16
Gorgonzola	31	Medium-fat blue cheese	16
Mascarpone	48	Low-fat cream cheese	16
Mozzarella	19	Feta	11
Parmesan	26	¼ cup grated Parmesan + ¼ cup breadcrumbs	Approx. 15
Meat, fish, game		**Meat, fish, game**	
Breast of lamb	37	Shoulder/leg of lamb	18
Lamb chop with fat	32	Lamb chop without fat, filet of lamb	28
Stewing chicken	20	Chicken breast	6
		Chicken leg/thigh	11
		Turkey	2–5

* Contained in 3.5 oz of the corresponding consumable food

High-Fat Food	Fat Content in g*	Low-Fat Food	Fat Content in g*
Beef brisket	15	Beef tenderloin	5
Pork shoulder	23	Pork loin	2
Sausages and meat products		**Sausages and meat products**	
Bacon, streaky	35	Lean, smoked ham	3
Salami	33	Turkey-salami	2
Ham, raw, medium-fat	33	Ham, raw, lean	2–3
Fish		**Fish**	
Salmon	13	Trout, pike, cod, pollock, haddock	1
Tuna packed in oil	22	Tuna packed in water	1
Tuna, raw	16	Swordfish	7
Oil, fats, nuts, seeds		**Oil, fats, nuts, seeds**	
Butter Oil	83 91	Medium-fat margarine	24
Nuts	50–60	Croutons, dry-toasted Wheat germ	15 10
Fruit, vegetables		**Fruit, vegetables**	
Olives, black	36	Olives, green	13
Grains		**Grains**	
Rolled oats	8	Cornflakes Whole-wheat flakes	0.7 2
* Contained in 3.5 oz of the corresponding consumable food			

Using this Index

To help you find recipes containing certain ingredients more quickly, this index also lists favorite ingredients (such as shrimp and bell peppers) in **bold type**, followed by the corresponding recipes.

ABBREVIATIONS

lb = pound
oz = ounce
tsp = teaspoon
tbs = tablespoon

The Author

Erika Casparek-Türkkan has been a journalist and cookbook author specializing in health and fitness for many years. As editor of a health magazine, she headed the food and nutrition department for a number of years and wrote books on healthy ways to lose weight. She also dedicates more and more of her time to her two hobbies —traveling and cooking. This has contributed to her vast appreciation of international recipes.

The Photographer

Jörn Rynio works as a photographer in Hamburg, Germany. His customers include national and international magazines, book publishers, and ad agencies. All the recipe photos in this book were produced in his studio with the enthusiastic support of his food stylist, Martina Mehldau

Photo Credits

FoodPhotographie Eising, Martina Görlach: cover photo
All others: Jörn Rynio, Hamburg

Published originally under the title Clay Pot Low Fat—viel Aroma auf leichte Art © 2002 Gräfe und Unzer Verlag GmbH, Munich. English translation for the U.S. market © 2003, Silverback Books, Inc.

Editor: Jonathan Silverman, Beate Pfeiffer
Translator: Christie Tam
Reader: Adelheid Schmidt-Thomé
Proofreader: Elizabeth Penn
Typesetting and production: Patty Holden
Layout, typography and cover design: Independent Medien Design, Munich

Printed in Korea

ISBN 1-930603-37-1

Editions: 5th (2006) 4th (2005), 3rd (2004), 2nd (2003), 1st (2002)

Enjoy Other Quick & Easy Books

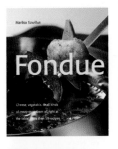

Marlisa Szwillus
Fondue
Cheese, vegetables, all kinds of meat—cook them all right at the table. More than 50 recipes

Cornelia Adam
Salads
An array of salads to eat as appetizers, entrées, and party dishes. Includes classic choices and cutting-edge alternatives.

Sandwiches
Store-bought and homemade breads and rolls combine with classic and new fillings.

Xenia Burgtorf

Cornelia Adam
Quiche
Delicious, savory pies with vegetables, meat, poultry or fish—serve for all occasions

Cornelia Adam
Garlic
Sophisticated recipes with the favorite Spice of the Mediterranean. Blustery or Spicy (tangy), Fine (delicate), International

Cornelia Schinharl
Easy Vegetarian
Uncomplicated and sophisticated — Vegetarian recipes for all seasons

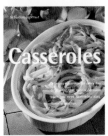

Sebastian Dickhaut
Casseroles

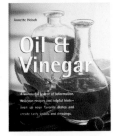

Annette Heisch
Oil & Vinegar
A wonderful source of information, delicious recipes and helpful hints— liven up your favorite dishes and create tasty sauces and dressings.

Andreas Fürtmayr
Sushi
Classic ideas from Japan and new fusion sushi. Home-made perfectly.

1 Noodle, 50 Sauces
Everyday Pasta • Old and New Italian Dishes
Noodle biography • 10 Tips for Success

Healthy Wok
Elisabeth Döpp
Christian Willrich
Jaen Rehne

Great for light and satisfying meals

Antje Gruener
Grilling

Gina Greifenstein
1 Batter— 50 Cakes
Baking to your heart's content

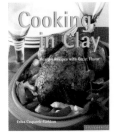

Cooking in Clay
Healthy Recipes with Great Flavor

Erika Casparek-Türkkan

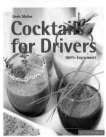

Doris Muliar
Cocktails for Drivers
100% Enjoyment

Antipasti and Tapas
Mediterranean Appetizers
Cornelia Schinharl

Soups
Classic to Contemporary

Sebastian Dickhaut

Claudia Schmidt
Raclette
New Recipes with Cheese Primer and Party Dips

LOW-FAT DISHES

➤ So you want low-fat cuisine? No problem with the clay pot! You can prepare any dish without fat.

➤ Although fat contributes to the flavor, you can also make dishes tasty with a clever use of herbs and spices.

➤ To round out the flavor and maximize the health benefits of fat-soluble vitamins, you can add a little fat to a finished dish.

Guaranteed Success with Your Clay Pot

CLAY POT AND MICROWAVE

➤ These two appliances can be fine complements to one another. First thaw frozen foods in the microwave and then cook them in the clay pot. If the clay pot fits inside the microwave, you can presoak it and use it in the microwave for thawing, then place it in an oven preheated to 250°F before increasing the heat.

JUICY MEAT

➤ Wrap or cover lean roasts with vegetable leaves to keep them juicy. For example, blanch cabbage or leeks shortly beforehand so the leaves are softer and easier to work.

SIDE DISHES

➤ Take advantage of the hot oven and cook the side dishes alongside the clay pot. For recipes and tips, see page 9. Naturally, you can also cook other dishes such as potatoes au gratin.